The Pen & The Lens

The Pen & The Lens

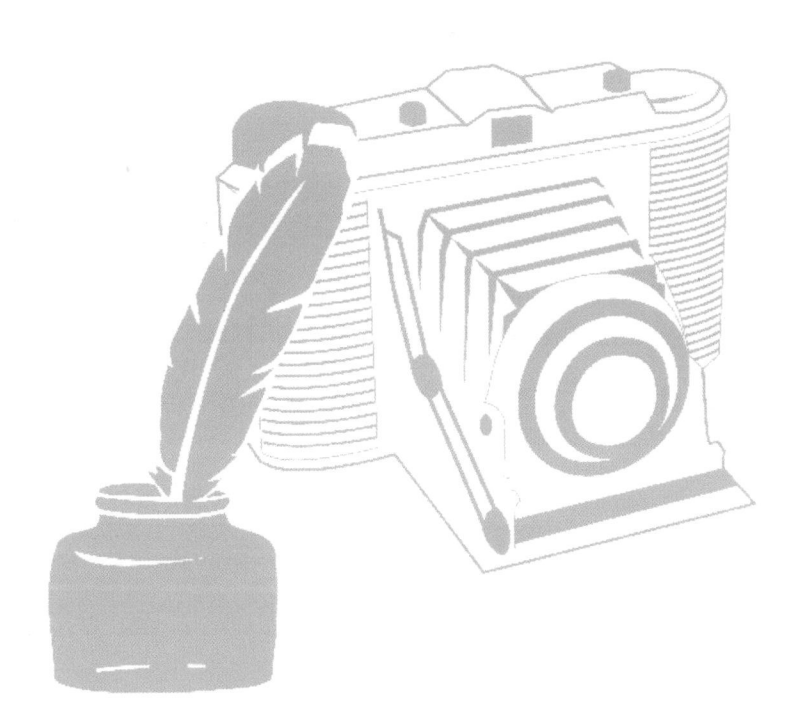

The Pen and The Lens

Author:	Anthony C. Gruppo
Photography:	Jemma M. McCarthy
Cover Art:	Bogdan Albu
Contributing Editor:	Caryn Ojeda
Editor:	Jesse Ojeda
Production Editor:	Shannon Peel

The scanning, uploading, and distribution of this book via the internet or via any other means without permission of the publisher is illegal. Please purchase only authorized electronic editions and do not participate in or encourage electronic piracy of copyright materials. Your support of the author's rights is appreciated.

ISBN: 978-0-9991471-2-2
© Copyright 2021
Anthony C. Gruppo & Jemma M. McCarthy

No parts of this publication may be reproduced digitally or non-digitally without the expressed permission of the Publisher:

Published By:

MarketAPeel
939 Homer Street
Vancouver, BC
V6B 2W6

Anthony C. Gruppo's share of the proceeds of *The Pen and The Lens* will be donated to Autism Research.

Table of Contents

Introduction	9
The Pen	10
The Lens	12
Above All Else	16
Just in Time Valentine	18
The Flexible Flyer	20
The Keys to the Castle	22
Shores of the Soul	24
Gazes & Glances	26
Moments & Momentum	28
The Black Stone	30
The Outer Shell	32
The Spirit Wolf	34
The Mystical Safari	36
The Hidden Cottage	38
Night Diver	40
Shard of Class	42
Into the Portal	44
Servant Leader	46
Waking Whisper	48
Web of Wonder	50

The Bare Facts	52
The Child Truth	54
Peace Cove	56
The Endless Track	58
The Bridge	60
Shadow Dancer	62
One Solitary Soul	64
Peck's Pond	66
Four Seasons of Forgotten	68
The Pretend Bike	70
The Smallest Window	72
Passage Promise	74
Scotland	76
Destiny Imagination	78
Cathedrals and Clouds	80
The Grove and the Cutter	82
The Grandest Children	84
A Dog's Reign	86
The Distance Runner	88
See Sounds	90
London Speaks	92
Almost Home	94
Other Books	96
Pen & Lens Reflections	101

The Pen & The Lens

The Pen & The Lens

My poetry is our shared journey through life. The Pen and the Lens is a book of my poetry about, love, romance, family, loss, sacrifice, career, society, and leadership. My poetry is for everyone because it is about everyone. My international journey is the canvas for my poetry, and in it, beats the hearts of those I love, those I have lost and those I have come to know and cherish. Everyone who has ever had to say goodbye to a loved one whether for career travel or the circle of life will feel connected through my poems. I want to express my gratitude to Jemma for bringing my poems to life through her photography. Her artistry captures the emotion within the poems. So travel with me now and together may we experience the beauty of life and humanity.

The Pen

Anthony C. Gruppo is an American author, poet and international executive. Anthony has faced first-hand the many challenges of accomplishing achievement in life. In the hardworking rural towns of Pennsylvania, amidst the boundless pace and energy of New York City, the breadth and scope of Texas, the eclectic Californian lifestyle, the diversity of Southeast Florida and the cultural wonder of the United Kingdom. His poetry is an expression of personal gratitude to all those who have moved him… and shaped his life.

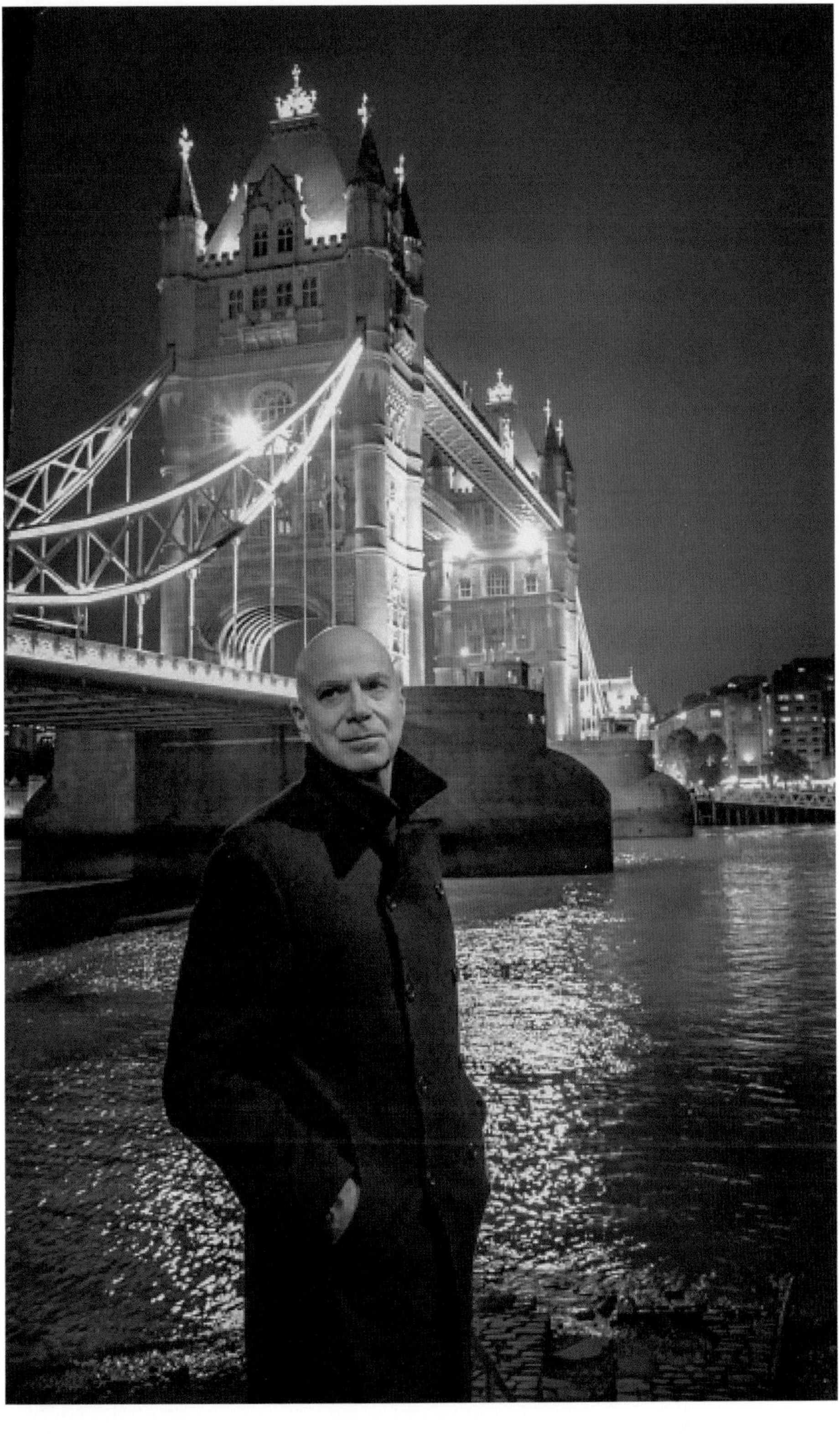

The Lens

Jemma M. McCarthy is a British photographer featured on the BBC, and other national publications and media. Jemma finds her creative inspiration from her life as an adventurer. She has cycled and hiked in exotic locations from rough camping in the Serengeti to cycling the paddy fields of Vietnam, the idyllic islands of Thailand and throughout Europe. Her adventures and creativity intersect as she captures the essence and emotion of the poetry.

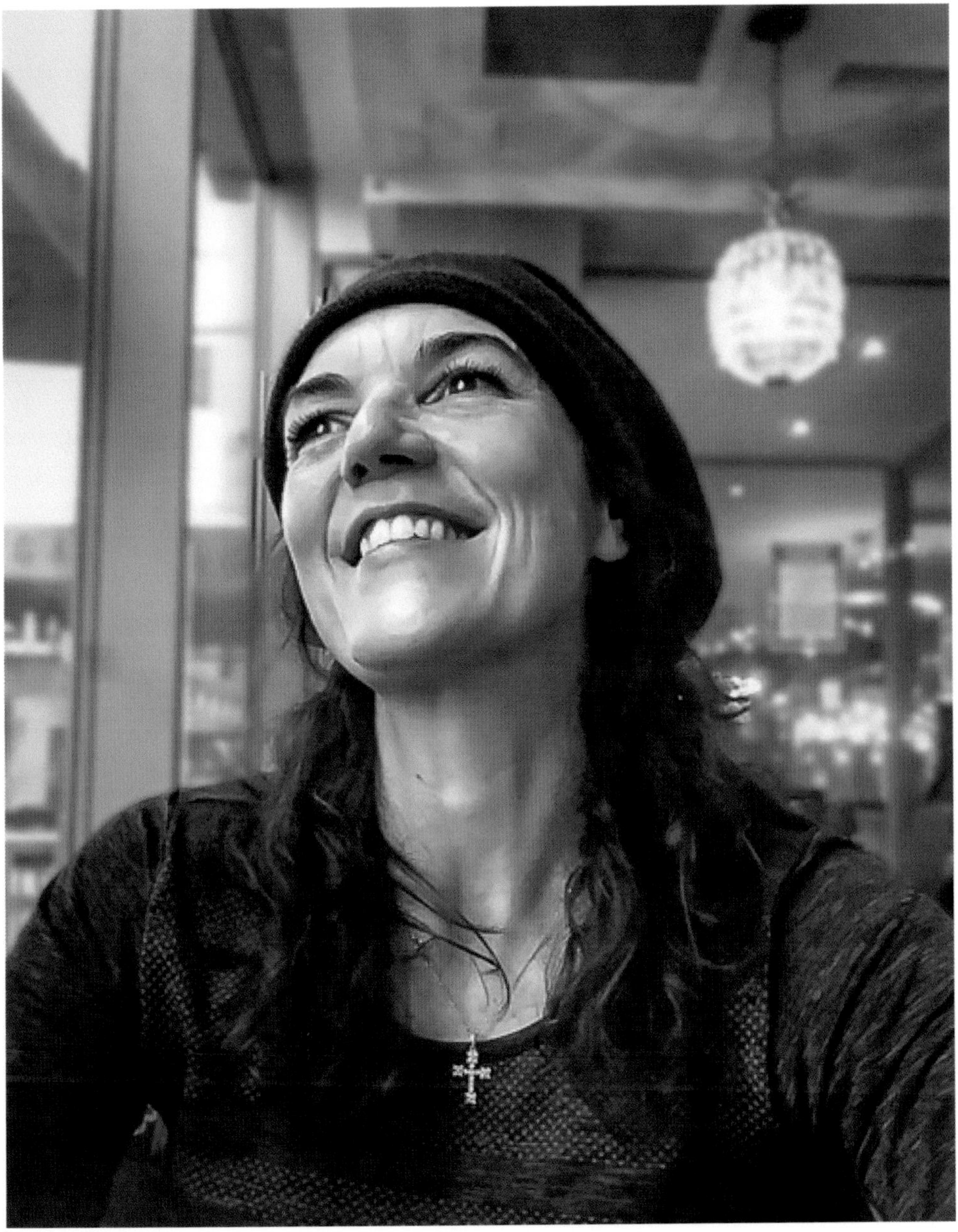

The Pen & The Lens

Above All Else

It takes such little height to stand so tall,
Brothers entwined rising above the wall.
A burden of barriers placed before them rise up,
Please take a long drink from the acceptance cup.

See in their eyes how strong and so wise,
Never break their future and force them to compromise.
Above all else see us together in a global piggyback,
Honor each other above all else and not the white or black.

With bare feet we were born and learned to take a first step,
Above all else, be a citizen of the world and do not sidestep.
Let us carry the brother when others grow weary,
Above all else find the way to comfort the teary.

We can create the dream where brothers can play,
A humanity of together molded from within our clay.
Look at their eyes and the vision above all else,
This weight is for us to carry, not only someone else.

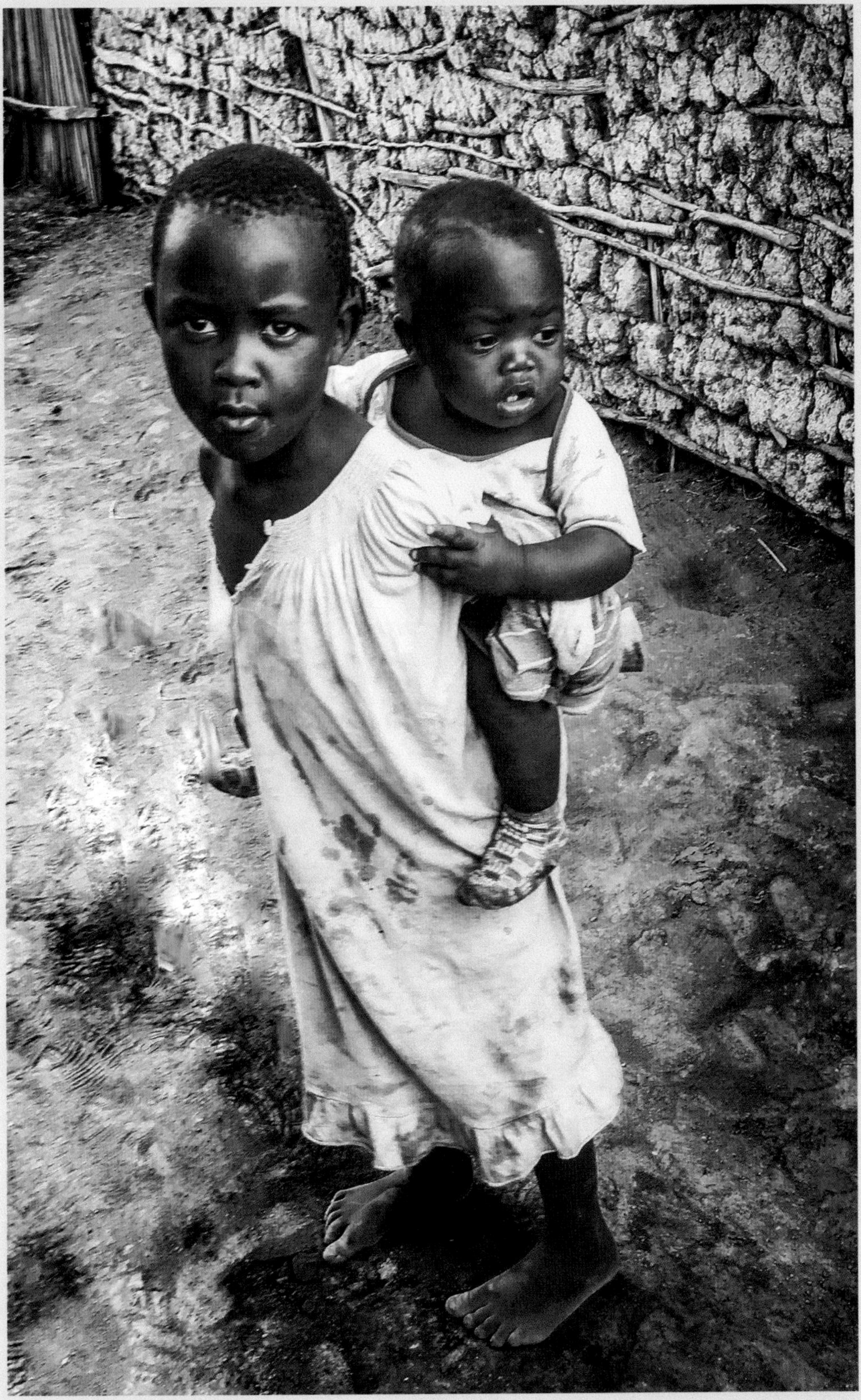

Just in Time

The old man sits bedside holding her weak hand.
The smell of the final flower enters his senses.
The memory of their passion stems like a rose.
Just in Time Valentine.

The schoolgirl hands out her Valentine's Day cards.
Saving the special one for the boy in the back row.
He ignores her glance and grabs the glittering paper.
Just in Time Valentine.

The distant couple separated by work send a text.
Trying to make this one matter more than the others.
Words and pictures fill the memo line.
Just in Time Valentine.

She inspires him to do better
without a flower, note or comment.
Inspiration is the sharpest arrow of Cupid.
Just in Time Valentine.

The heart is the stopwatch to the soul.
It sets the pace and makes the promise.
Love wanders through time seeking
moments, they both matter only to each other.
Just in Time Valentine.

The old man cannot keep his eyes off of her.
Adoration as intense as that day long ago.
Romance is the intersection of inspiration and admiration.
Just in Time Valentine.

A couple smiles as they pass on the street.
A rose lies on her desk drying as does her tears.
Dinner concludes with a brief embrace.
Old and young remain in place.
Just in Time Valentine.

She closes her eyes for the final time.
Alas, his rose has wilted in his hand.
The hospital bed becomes the last vase.
He bows his head and looks to the window,

The dashing young man replaced with memories crashing.
He utters a final phrase to her resting soul:
You are My Sweetheart.
Out of Time Valentine.

THE FLEXIBLE FLYER

The boy learned to fly on the snow-covered hill,
Under him the Flexible Flyer Christmas sled.
Boots, gloves and hat drying on the radiator,
His mother baking raisin bread in the kitchen.

The man flying across the cloud covered sky,
Under him the jet sled of business hills.
His luggage and coat placed neatly above in the overhead,
His mother's raisin bread invades his senses.

Flexible manner the secret to opening adventures,
The passage of time as quick as the sled ride.
Metal blades and shoe leather keep the pace and place,
The Flexible Flyer can always smell the raisin bread in his movement.

Boyhood memories create flexible flying successes and failures,
Doors open to see first snow and first dreams.
One cannot quit the climb of the hill no matter the depth of snow and challenge.
The mother passed; the raisin bread ceased to bake but the man believed.

The sounds of a life sledding over the glade of forever trying to speed up,
The crust of hard snow and hard challenges crunching away the years.
The snow shall fall again as will some of his endeavors,
Raisin bread bakes in his memories seeing a mother's smile.

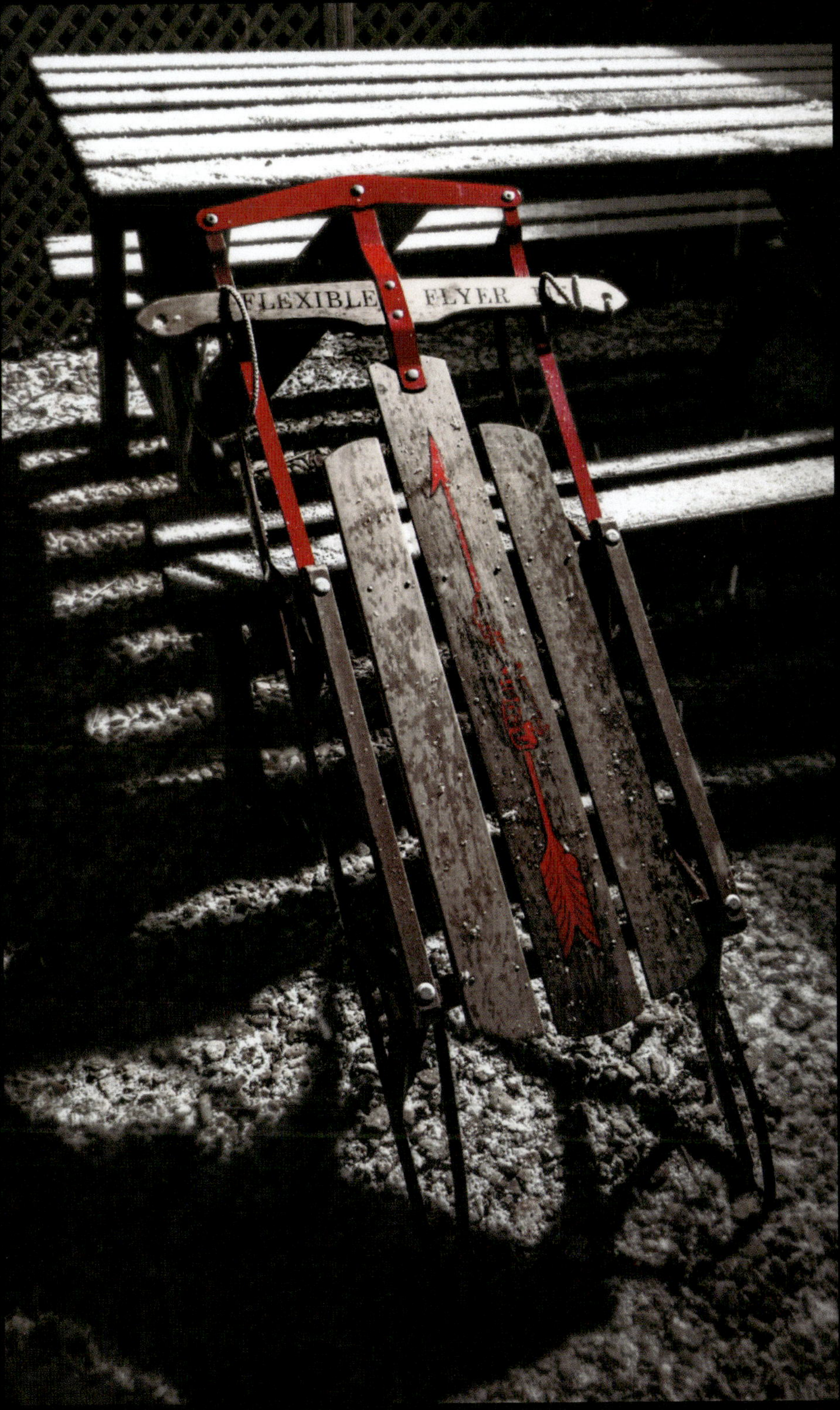
FLEXIBLE FLYER

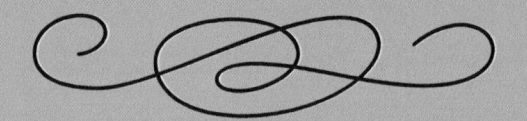

The Keys to The Castle

In the dimly lit room she touches the keys,
Her mind a blade sharpening on the task.
She works at home providing him an edge,
In moments the answers so wise escape her lips.

For what is love if not the keys to the castle?
A castle of talent surrounded by beauty.
Her fingers touch the puzzle pieces on an ancient desk,
Eager to build a bridge over the moat of his troubles.

He lovingly watches her think with a soft smile,
Immersed in her calm mind and focus of instinct.
For what is love if not their living mirror of one another?
The glaring reflection what others cannot see.

Pressure consumes him for decisions he must make and those to come,
What use are the keys to the castle if not to unlock the dream?
The turn of the lock is not an opening to tomorrow,
It was and always will be the threshold to their escape.

For you see, she was always the key to the castle,
A simple and quiet place to behold.
The castle made of brick and mortar of mortality,
He lived to return and reside inside her fortress of forever.

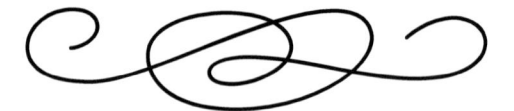

The sounds of river and wind dance upon the floor of tomorrow.
A whisper of voices far away tell the secrets of waves to come.
Children skip rocks as the ripples roll slow enough for laughter.
Carving the banks of the river standing tall against the wind.

Can a boat of burden-laden sacrifice sail on the seas of care?
He stares out praying to see the shores of soul once again.
Religion is not the only prayer book for a guide in turbulent waters.
Shores of rock and sand, whether brown or white, call the landing.

The tide is a mere tickle under the feet of responsibility,
Duty and role lash themselves to the crow's nest sighting the family land.
Wind and rain pelt the promise of an end to the voyage,
The shore looms ahead, a mere pier where souls can dance.

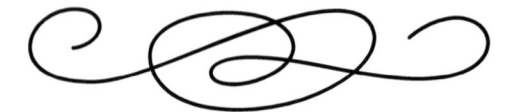

Shores of the Soul

GAZES & *Glances*

Gazes and glances see beyond the heart's blind eye,
A spiritual blend of inquisitive minds refusing to see the elusive why.
Created path of personal cobblestones linking the fame,
No gaze or glance over the shoulder can envision what is not tame.

Fortune and fame written on crumpled pages,
The desire to make a difference upon the ages.
Lovers and loners, a club of members
Used up gazes and glances singed in the embers.

Remember the times when time stood still
A field, a forest, an old lumber mill.
Gazes and glances transcend the ground,
Waking up each morning and loving her around.

Some have left and you miss them so,
Counting blessings as the little souls grow.
Gazes and glances see around the bend,
Where age and faith are on the mend.

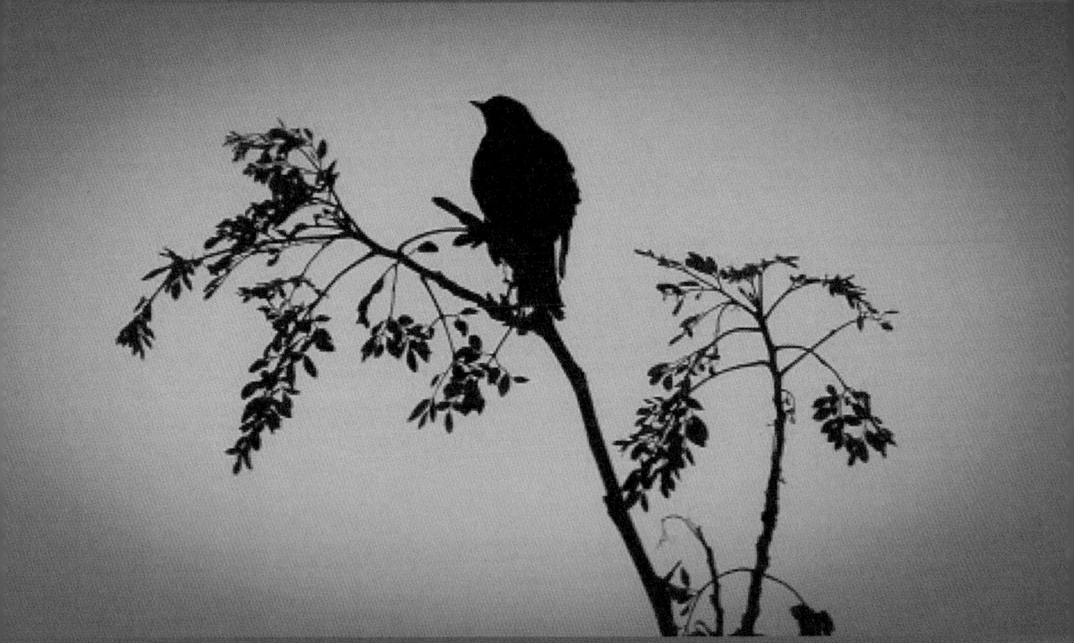

Moments
&
Momentum

Look into the eyes to journey inside,

Feel the moves of momentum to begin the ride.

Warrior strength both gifted and strong,

Within lies the chorus of your personal song.

Your heart is a clock of ring and chime,

The constant movement like a poet's rhyme.

Never too little and never too much,

Find the answer that comes without touch.

Live your story, break the chains and beat the odds,

It takes no bricks, steel or concrete rods.

Become the flag placed at the summit of a personal mountain,

Where you exhale your breath from the internal fountain.

Courage and honor when brought through sin,

You can see where you have never been.

Soon the momentum of moments will have come and gone,

Those memories and marks of legacy chiseled in stone.

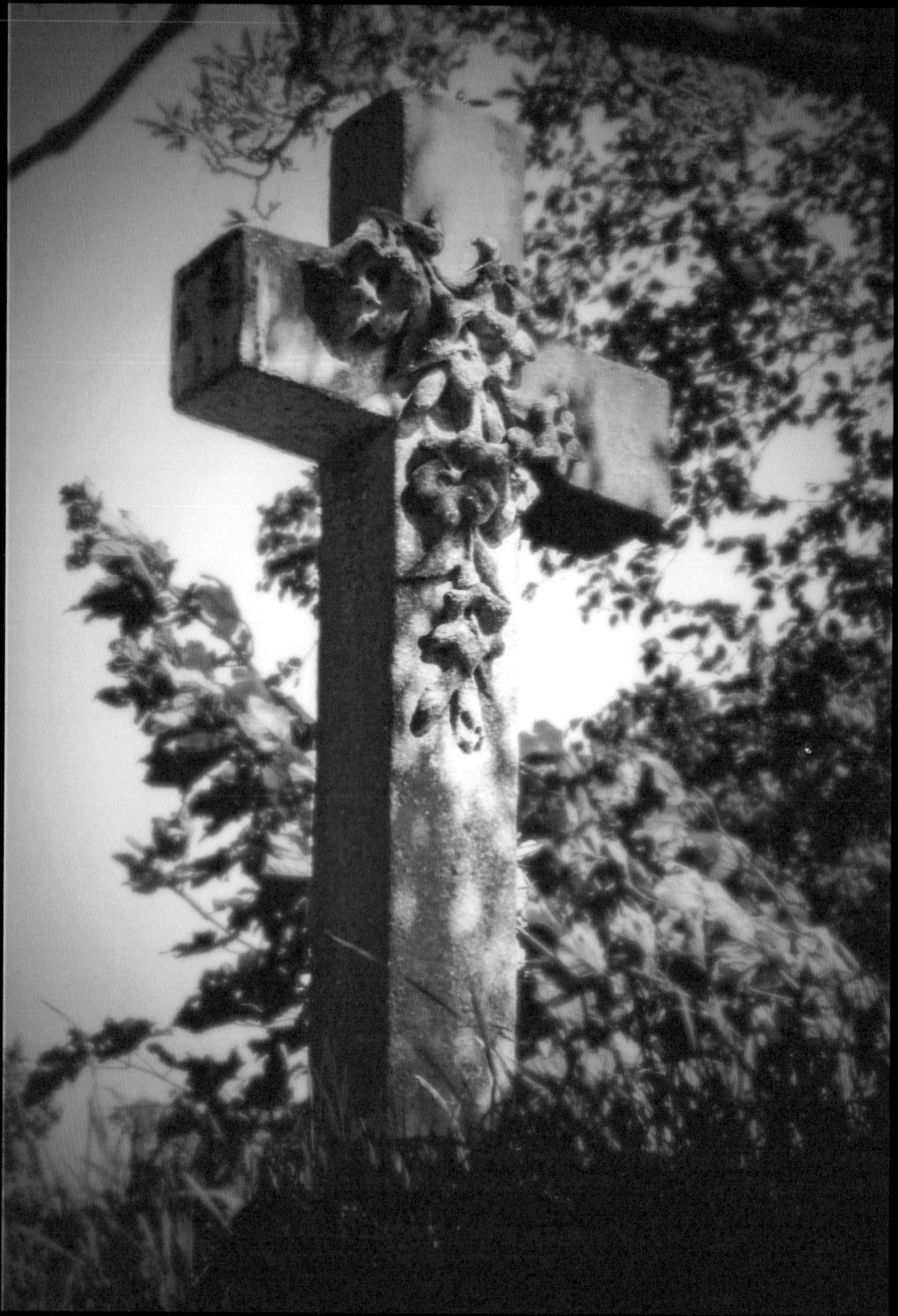

The Black Stone

Together they lie near the black stone while gazing from the sky,
A mother and father visited in memories after we said goodbye.
Time talks in the mind of the boy they guided from birth,
The sacrifices made when they were children of worth.

Photos and frames filled with family history and smiles,
The struggles they endured while love walked the miles.
Visits and calls now seem so distant when standing at the stone,
Perhaps the pain of loss, their boy would have to own.

Each Memorial Day the parents walked with their daughter and son,
To visit the stones of their family where the legacy had begun.
You hear the prayers sprinkled among the wreaths and flowers,
Just wanting to see them again and hold on tight for a few hours.

So you call your son and your daughter to drink in their sound,
While keeping a hand on the black stone in the ground.
The mountain stands guard over the parent's place of rest,
You hear their words of encouragement to become the best.

For all their humble living and loving those two stood tall,
Raising a family made of their strong stone to bear it all.
The black stone is but a marker to remain in place,
You merely need to envision them to have them in your space.

The time will arrive when your son and daughter will stand,
Listening to the prayers at the black stone feeling your distant hand.
What happiness will arise from the memory of the joy and laughter,
It was the love and continuation of the generations they were after.

The Outer Shell

Her outer shell is so alluring, a gorgeous womanly cover.

The real longing is her inner beauty, that which most fail to uncover.

The brash and rash who judge with rules,

They lose her personality and poise, oh what fools!

Most travel a path laden with their hollow pledges,

Standing with her greatness, no need to fear life's ledges.

A picture of her fills the pages,

A life with her is happiness for the ages.

Smart and wise, I seek her opinion,

She is worthy of honor and never someone's minion.

Trying to stay near while still distant,

Trusting her instincts in an instant.

Outer shells are temporary and may leave us,

Her spirit and energy so worth the fuss.

Jealousy and weakness may try to attack,

She is the ultimate friend who has your back.

For me, I intend to know her better,

In person, by phone or even a letter.

For you who cannot see past her shell,

I wish you a speedy trip to hell.

The Spirit Wolf

Sound of a faint howl reaches the spirit totem,
The shadow of the Wolf encircles the fire.
The embers lick the edges of instinct and trust,
Wolf reminds the loner to return to the pack.

A physical form takes shape in the dream,
Visions of intuition and perception of his kind.
Raw emotion threatens the body and spirit,
Losing patience with sheep who inhabit the field.

The appetite for freedom claws the ground,
Not easily domesticated to conformity and rules.
Wolf reluctantly attends the tribal ceremony,
Warning the spirit to beware and refuse to comply.

The Wolf seeks competition within their own pack,

Behaviors of spirit bounding away from the boundaries.

Intuitive landscape, the wolf's personal domain,

Passion to prance to the dangerous edge.

Spirit Wolf and the truth are one in the same,

The shadow comes and the reality grows.

Never separated is the spirit from company of the Wolf,

Perhaps the final act of a totem timepiece.

The Mystical Safari

The mind travels where only the heart can lead,
Safari of spirit awakened by the sunrise of mystical beginnings.
Thoughts like wild animals thunder over the creative awareness,
Searching for the perfect combination of elegance and energy.

Magical sunrises appear in the horizon of dreamscapes,
The rolling of a mind and body like a log trapped at the waterfall.
Fragments of imagination run with the herd to reach high ground.
Mystical safari can see through the dust storm of adversity,
Walking a new blazed trail where possibility has yet to emerge.

Memory can feel what the mystical safari has revealed,
Tents of tenacity dot the edge of the wonderment wilderness.
Mystical safari is both imagined and real to touch and feel.
A journey of the mind freed from captivity of comfort.

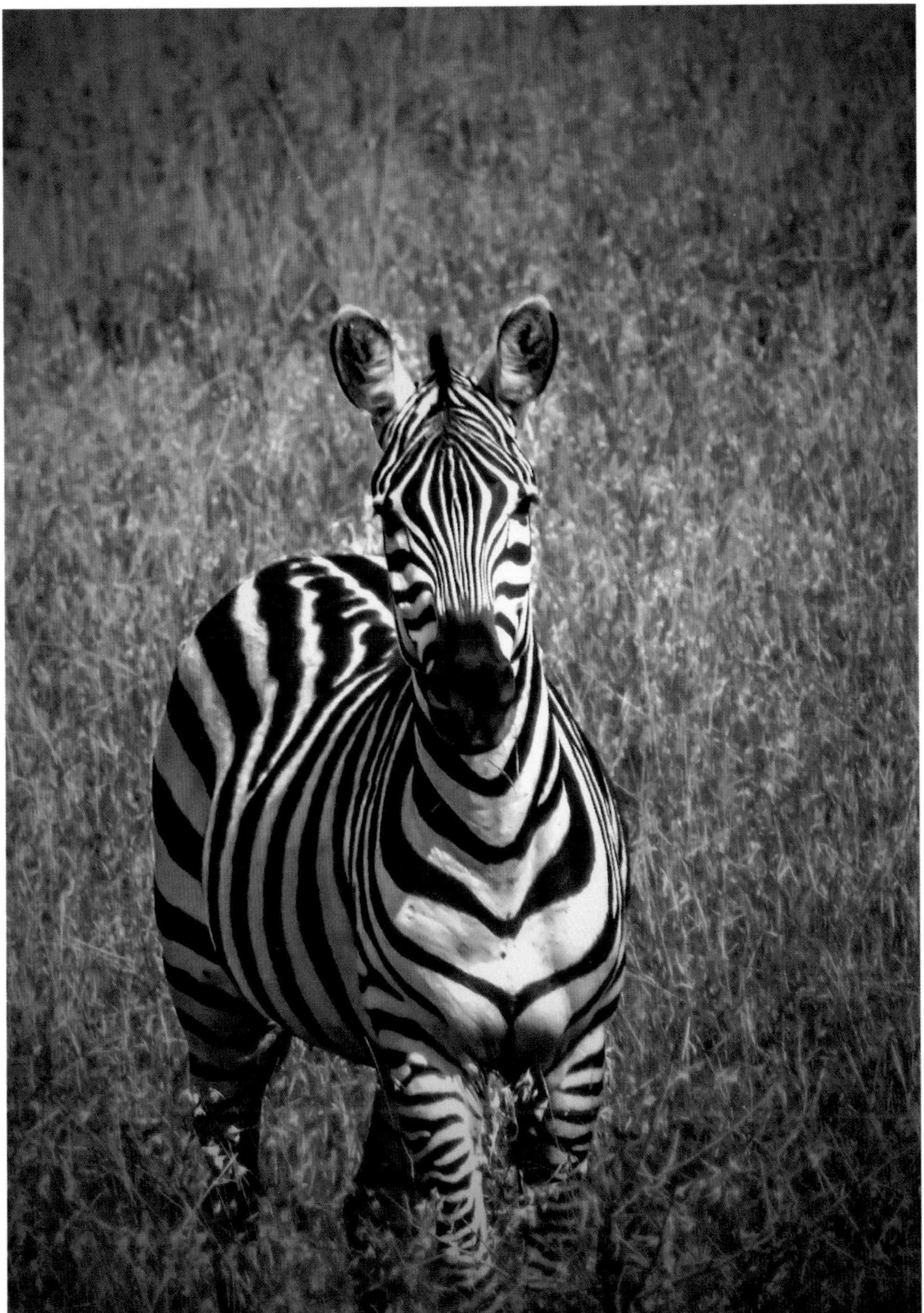

A deep feeling lies inside the tall grass growing outside,

Where our feelings have come to be hidden under a field of rock.

The years have driven us deeper and deeper against the base of the mountain,

The tranquility of living has yet to replace the regretful decisions.

Tiny windows open to view the majesty of moments,

Knowing there was always those who will come if we let them.

The hidden cottage, no matter how beautiful, is best inhabited by many,

A shingled roof and fireplace come together to gather the memories.

To find the hidden cottage, one must first find themselves,

Backpack of experiences hangs on the hook on the wall.

The musty smell of the forest welcomes the senses,

The hidden cottage unlocks where no chain was seen.

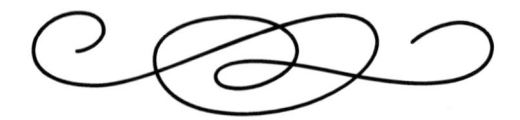

The Hidden Cottage

Night Diver

The ocean was peaceful as darkness covered the craft,

Divers quietly checking their gear, no one would laugh.

A deep blue Caribbean surf calling to them to be sure,

The peacefulness a treasure greater than pirate lure.

Night divers know the risk in their adventurous quest.

He straps his knife to his calf, inviting memories to be his guest.

Under the surface the men dive deep,

Thinking of those passed that swim in eternal sleep.

He surveys his gauges to determine his air,

Seaweed brushes him like the edge of a stair.

He levels the descent as the water becomes cold,

Recalling the stories of loved ones young and old.

Cautiously, the diver approaches the coral wall,

Several surprises can reside in this ocean stall.

Past and future steps invade his mind,

More powerful and lasting throughout all time.

His dive buddy shines a light on a creature,

Style and intellect illuminating a stunning feature.

The four decide to return to the surface,

All marine beauty and life is lived with purpose.

Night divers search the depths for the thrill,

Danger and challenge make time stand still.

He would be blessed to see today become tomorrow,

Life without chosen depth is the ultimate sorrow.

She rises above London as the epitome of class,
Sensing her immense presence from his balcony of balance and glass.
A landmark of living options housed inside the jagged edges,
The Thames waves to her from the rapid ride forming the ledges.

From a distant basin the Shard of class offers comfort.
A daily reminder of the distance one has travelled to see her standing effort.
Evening lights dance to the theme of a prominence of purpose retold,
City protected by her brilliant reach to where the sky can unfold.

A Shard of class holding court while guarding a storied tower and bridge,
Watching her bathed on the rain-soaked meditational ridge.
You come to know the first time you saw her the same as the last,
Always remembering this marvel of beauty, this Shard of class.

Shard of *Class*

into the
PORTAL

A secret door lies ready to open upon acceptance,
Knowledge of that acceptance is why you have come to the portal.
The transformation where internal fire fuels the ultimate belief,
Faith and belief are the map inside the portal to the natural state of yourself.

Portals will find you when you least expect them to appear,
The readiness to travel to the understanding of the "where" and "why".
It was there where you sought to travel in the depth of the mind,
A mind expanding to accept and alter what the portal would share.

It is not some science or magic to land where the portal sends you,
There where the acceptance, awareness and transformation could live.
As the portal closes and the inner travel begins to set its course,
You come to realize you were the portal of self-transformation.

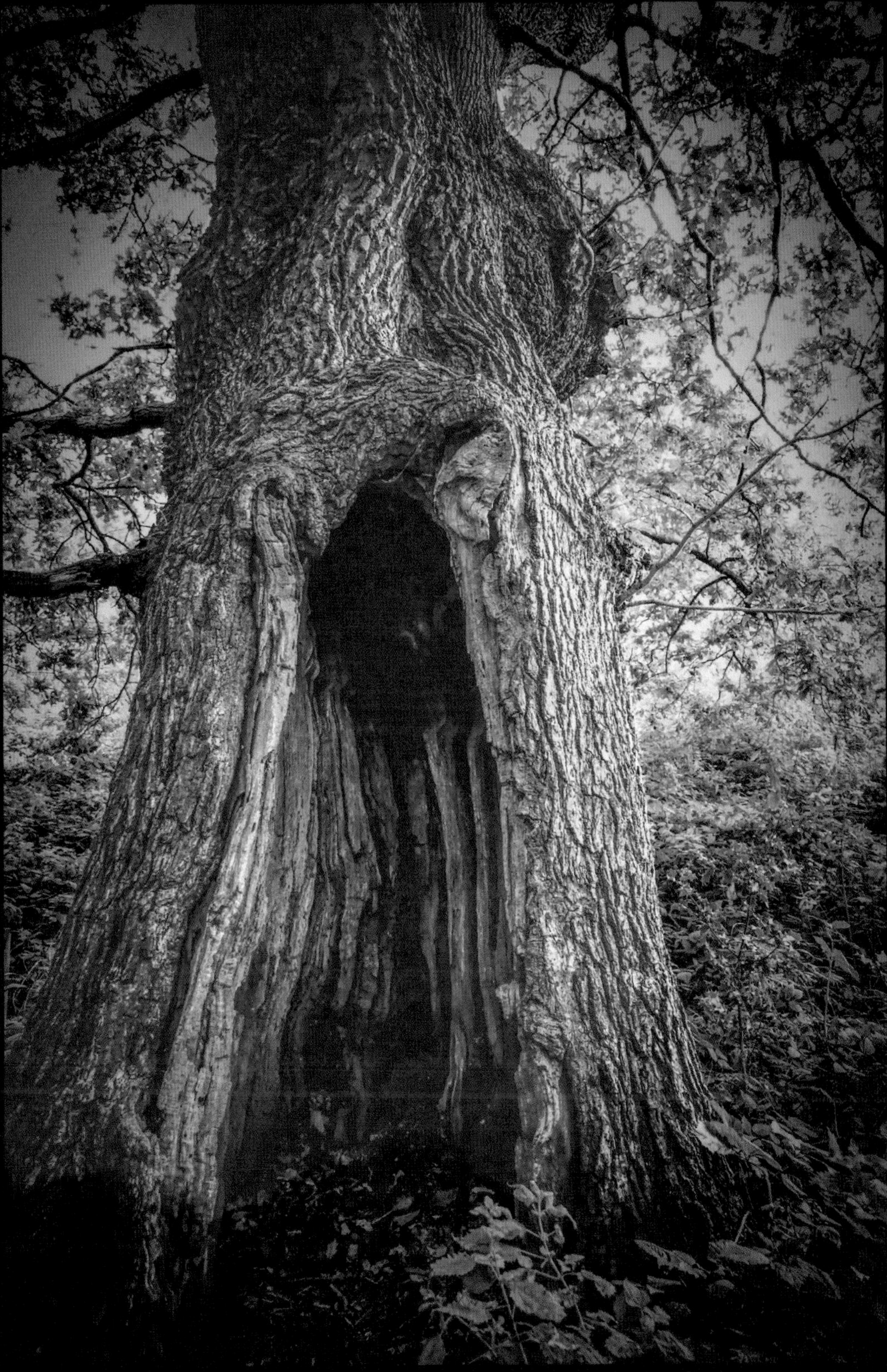

Servant Leader

The loneliness of command hardens the human steel,
A thought of decision cast upon a spinning wheel.
For those who pray for hope and eternal salvation,
Learning to live and serve with care erases all internal damnation.

Within the matrix of math and methods, ambition calls:
Where are the people who stood in the changing halls?
The servant leads within the challenges of a structured land,
Fearless in the pursuit of the ultimate mission to lend a hand.

It was never his to own and alter their fate,
A guardian of tomorrow opening the gate.
Many shall forget the face and name,
Of the servant whom roamed, that host of the game.

When you see the history of the pledge,
The driven focus to survive on the edge.
It was you he loved and not a vision,
To serve the impossible moment, his final mission.

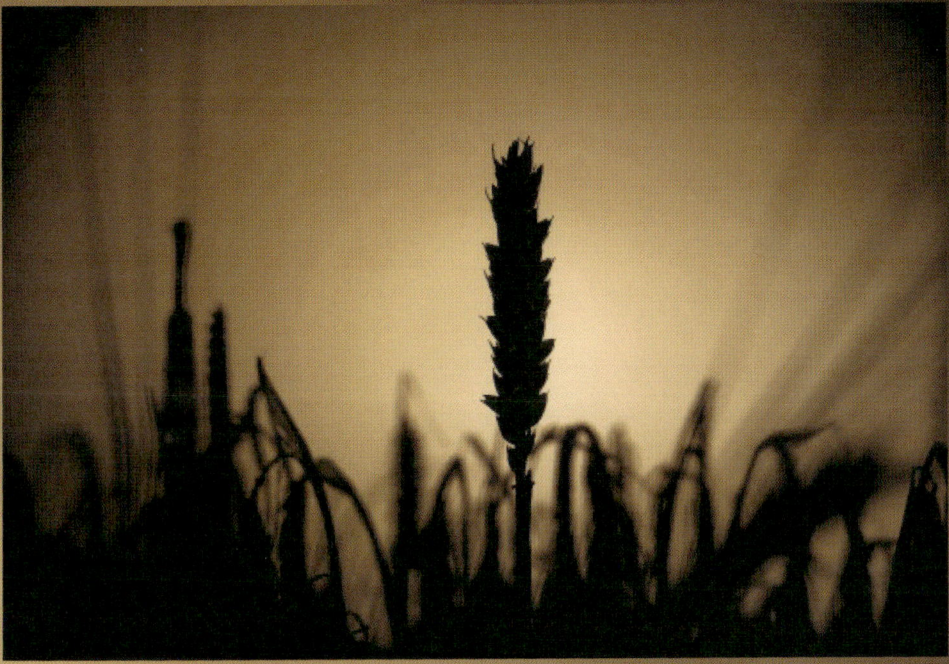

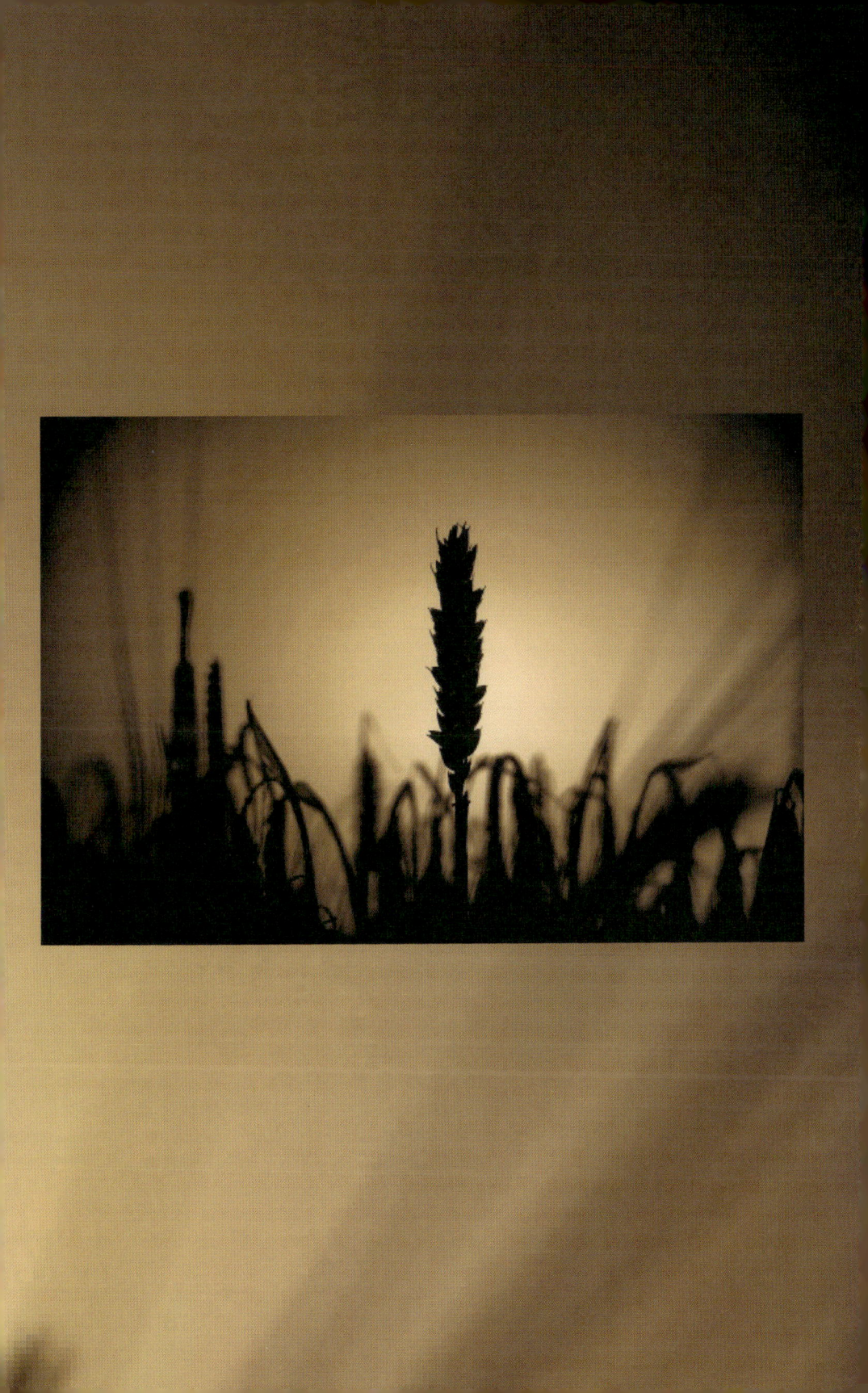

First sunlight rejoices seeing the waking whisper ignite.

Another whisper of waking from the sleepless night.

Possessing the heart to walk into the light,

Energy-filled charm begins to take flight.

A slim silhouette of shadow understood by so few,

Every tree, rock, and hill pleads to serve as our pew.

Knowing the most powerful prayer created in nature's church,

This waking whisper of promise bends a knee on life's perch.

A smile which defines the arts of living and love,

Nature greets the waking whisper like a peaceful dove.

When the mind struggles to separate mission from ambition,

One seeks a magical whisper longing to inhale the premonition.

Waking whisper of thought lies on a personal page,

A timeless beauty of entirety and grace void of age.

Let us all listen for the whispering voice of tomorrow,

The waking whisper of wonder for us all to borrow.

Waking Whisper

Webs of wonder are spun from the life of belief,

A constant creation of desires and wires tightly bound.

The flexible feel of tangled emotion in a heart clawing to center,

The wondrous web of poetic promises in perfect symmetry.

To trap the love within the wonder web of romance,

Lovers like spiders encircling strands of vise-like grip.

Clear in color, the web of wonder paints a mosaic,

A picture of unity and birth of the couple's floating feelings.

Natural silk of the web knits the lovers strength of embrace,

Wonder webs arise to transport the lovers to shelter their senses.

They begged to be trapped and held by the care of a wedded web,

High above the ground of reality they are seen only by their web of wonder.

WEB OF WONDER

Touch and time age together to blur the bare facts,

The wiring of two intertwined souls beyond the folly of flesh.

Their energy shocks the senses when life tries to dull them.

Bare facts can be remembered even when memory is forced to fade,

The longing for the door to open when time travel loses its grip.

Theirs was entrapment of breath exhaled in a cloud of goodbyes.

The bare facts of belonging to each other when even the heavens beckoned,

A captured look which speaks loudly even though no words are heard.

A cascade of adventure inside a tiny space fueled with laughter.

Who were these bearers of the bare facts?

Will each, in turn, return to tell their story?

What matters to them is not the bare facts, but the bare belief in each other.

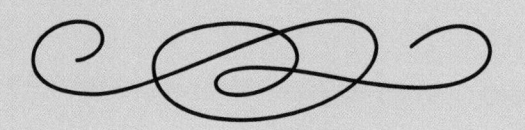

The Bare Facts

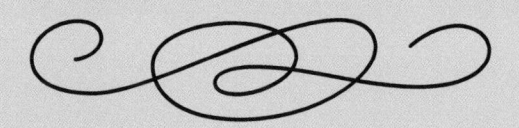

Children will play and laugh together regardless of race and religion,

Always seeing each other in every game and creative vision,

They embrace diversity like they embrace their family's love, where acceptance is alive.

The message children send to us to hear: please live together to truly thrive.

We all smile, looking upon the children telling their stories to each other.

The guiding light of acceptance, empowering us to love one another.

The child truth perhaps has been lost in the closed mind of nameless,

For our children accept each other into their playground of safeness.

We can let go, and become the student of the child teacher,

From all directions of an earth where equality of humanity is the preacher.

To anger and hate the sullen child takes witness,

A view into our racism and doubt we ask them to serve as eyewitness.

Children truth flows like a river through even the most troubled land,

They treasure their differences in appearance and upon love they stand.

Those who are blinded in unfounded fear of unknown people take heed,

For the answer to your awakening of truth lies in the children we need.

The Child Truth

The smell of morning tastes of the time of peace,
Family of swans waken in the watery cove and marsh.
Presence of peace keeps time to their preparations,
Stopping to watch the passerby's reflection in the water.

Ducks looking so calm on the surface with a difference underneath,
Moist stones with moss do their part to keep the cove in peace.
Every color of green spread across the cove's peaceful easel,
Reeds and weeds act as the brushes and bristles on the canvas cove,
A soft rain dances, rhythm beating in their drops like a drum.

A heron stands like a conductor on the stage of the cove,
Leaves floating by looking like boats for the little insects to ride.
So peaceful the phrases spoken by the inhabitants of the cove,
Harmony resides inside the peaceful, watery cove of the memory.

Peace COVE

The endless track lies before you to explore your passion,

Train ride through inspiration seated where dreams find fashion.

Rails of metal bounce into the rutted rims of creativity connected,

While tunnels of time see the light of potential and curiosity neatly erected.

The station stop, an interruption to the endless track of found meaning,

Where the rider of reality holds onto the arm as the train starts leaning.

No crossing or intersection delays the travel along the endless track,

The lost moments of the past screaming to call the train back.

The turnstile awaits as the rider exits the final stop on the way,

Never can the endless track be denied an adventure today.

The conductor walks and nods as she points to the street,

Another endless track of tomorrow pounding like a heartbeat.

The ENDLESS TRACK

A mist anoints the motion as the bridge comes into view,

Crossing the ancient span where the world breathes anew.

Towers reaching from rapid river depths unfold the mystery,

Centuries and centurions float past her arches of history.

Sights and sounds across an ocean crash into formation,

Life and adventure crafted from challenge become the creation.

Wicked tides rise and fall, capturing the heartbeat of travel,

One trying not to succumb and surrender and ever unravel.

Wharfs like wizards cast their magic upon the traveler from shore,

Wind blows and howls while the waves dance confused and unsure.

Flexible is the traveler as the adventure takes flight,

Knowing the unknown is certain to visit when the sun shines bright.

Fog appears to block the balance of understanding now and however.

While the bridge battles, holding on tight to the sanctity of forever,

Boats and barges ask permission to pass under her stance.

Memories and momentum collide in unison to sing and dance.

The vision of possible, the bridge silently speaks her own name,

Adventurer and traveler on the final road of pressure-filled fame.

Stories are told and myths of mysteries creak from every direction,

The bridge will wave goodbye and be remembered with respect and affection.

The
Bridge

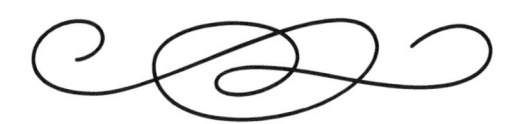

Music of motivation captures the silent shadow of a new dare,

An inspiring dance to move those who have ceased to care.

Shadow dancing on the floor of challenge enters the dream,

Where ambassadors of attitude have forsaken their role on the team.

This weight the shadow dancer must ultimately bear alone,

Floating shadows of doubt missing a step where results are unknown.

From the shadows to the light the dancer can hear the sounds,

Faint fellow dancers start to spin and dip, smiling as they come around.

Picking partners in dance, the Shadow leads from the front,

Pressing and pulling the dancers, chasing the thrill of the hunt.

The music is not confined to the present where change is alive,

It surrounds the air of the dancers who are driven to break loose and thrive.

Shadow Dancers are called when the band has stopped playing,

Musicians of magic resurrecting fallen skills from decaying.

When the dance has stopped and the shadow dancer departs,

It leaves the floor of the possible energized with renewed hearts.

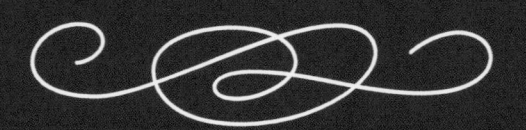

Shadow Dancer

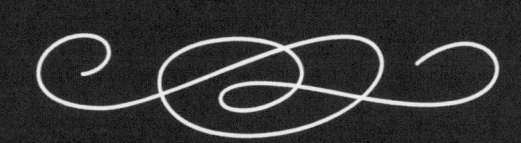

Crowds and the loud are deaf to a solitary soul standing still,

The breezes of the wind carrying the leaves of being alone.

Branches of strength support the isolation from the reborn roots,

Trunk of trial hardened by the abandonment of broken solo bark.

Solitary soul rising up from the pure virgin planted seed,

Fruit of toil is plucked from the single soul survivor of sacrifice.

A crowning of the tree made in the fight of the solitary life,

Twigs snap under the weight of the soul sounds crying for air.

One solitary soul gathers a crowd of flowering followers,

All yearning to climb the crafted ladder to the treehouse of turmoil.

Knowing the one soul has insight from inside the knothole of knowledge,

One game of solitaire left to be played in the final dealt hand.

1 Solitary *Soul*

One canoe slices through the thin layer of ice on the lake,

While a brisk breeze chills the face of the oarsmen as the craft glides.

A flying fish waves hello as it breaks the surface near the bow,

Even a beaver dam can be seen trying to slow the brook.

Silence, an eerie feeling of being watched as footsteps touch the forest floor,

White tails belonging to deer bounce away as the scent fills their noses.

A fox stares while keeping his distance from the two-legged visitor,

The climb becomes steeper as the trees become thinner and the rocks larger.

Above the ridge it all unfolds, where life is simple and complete,

Sitting to listen to the calm embrace of nature's creations.

Remaining still, the lives of the woods start to come closer,

If only this hidden magical world could avoid civilization.

Peck's Pond

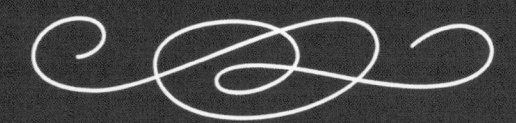

The air moves with the cold mists and momentum of the bold,

Two hearts connected, seeking to break the mould.

Where will she capture the new fallen snow?

Perhaps in a winter fire, burning what they know.

Forgotten are the changing tides and the bank of fall leaves,

the one man and woman stroll together and still believe.

Heavens of colour, the four seasons race on sky blue cloud,

Forever entangled, never forgotten, not when hearts beat loud.

The heat erodes as summer has left a barren land,

His senses forget the rain-soaked earth, but not her hand.

How stirring the passion to romance upon the end of the season,

No matter the challenge she will always be his reason.

They have outlasted the last and the night is still,

Senses collide with the passing power of will.

The four seasons of forgotten can clothe the hot ember,

Which warmed and protected what only those two shall remember.

4 Seasons of Forgotten

Rolled jean legs just above the ankle, a white T shirt over the top,
In the mind of the boy his bike a pretend chariot that could not be stopped.
A handmade sword of wood and screws held high to fight,
His small home, a pretend castle, disappears from sight.

The gravel road kicks a stone at his spokes and wheel,
But the pretend arrows of invisible enemies he does not feel.
He dismounts from his steed with rubber hoofs and lands on his feet.
Into the field the swashbuckler runs to perform a heroic feat.

The cyclist puts on the modern helmet and gear,
Harder to remember those pretend battles from a bygone year.
No sword, no shield as the aged rider changes speed,
Just one more imaginary adventure is what he may need.

The Pretend *Bike*

THE SMALLEST WINDOW

The traveler speeds above humanity.
The smallest window, the only view of earth's calamity.
Roads and towns in a woven grid.
Chariot of containment with a steel lid.

More times than remembered, strapped to a seat.
Deals and adventures flying to meet.
To the right, they read or sleep.
One old woman trying not to weep.

The memory of the yesterdays has started to fail.
Thunder in the sky, wind and the hail.
The engines roar with buzzing sound.
Hearts and feelings lost and found.

Eyes strain to view home.
Destined to fly, travel and roam.
The craft will bend, creak and lurch.
A prayer uttered from their sky church.

Consumed in clouds pitched to land.
The deal-makers circle to shake their hand.
Hands lift up the smallest window plastic shade.
Challenge and fortune to be made.

Sometimes they fail to matter in a day.
But in the sky, they cannot stay.
The chariot lowers and drops gear.
Smiling out the window without fear.

In distance from home there lies deep sorrow.
For a new smallest window departs tomorrow.
Those they love not aware of their loss.
The price without them, a great cost.

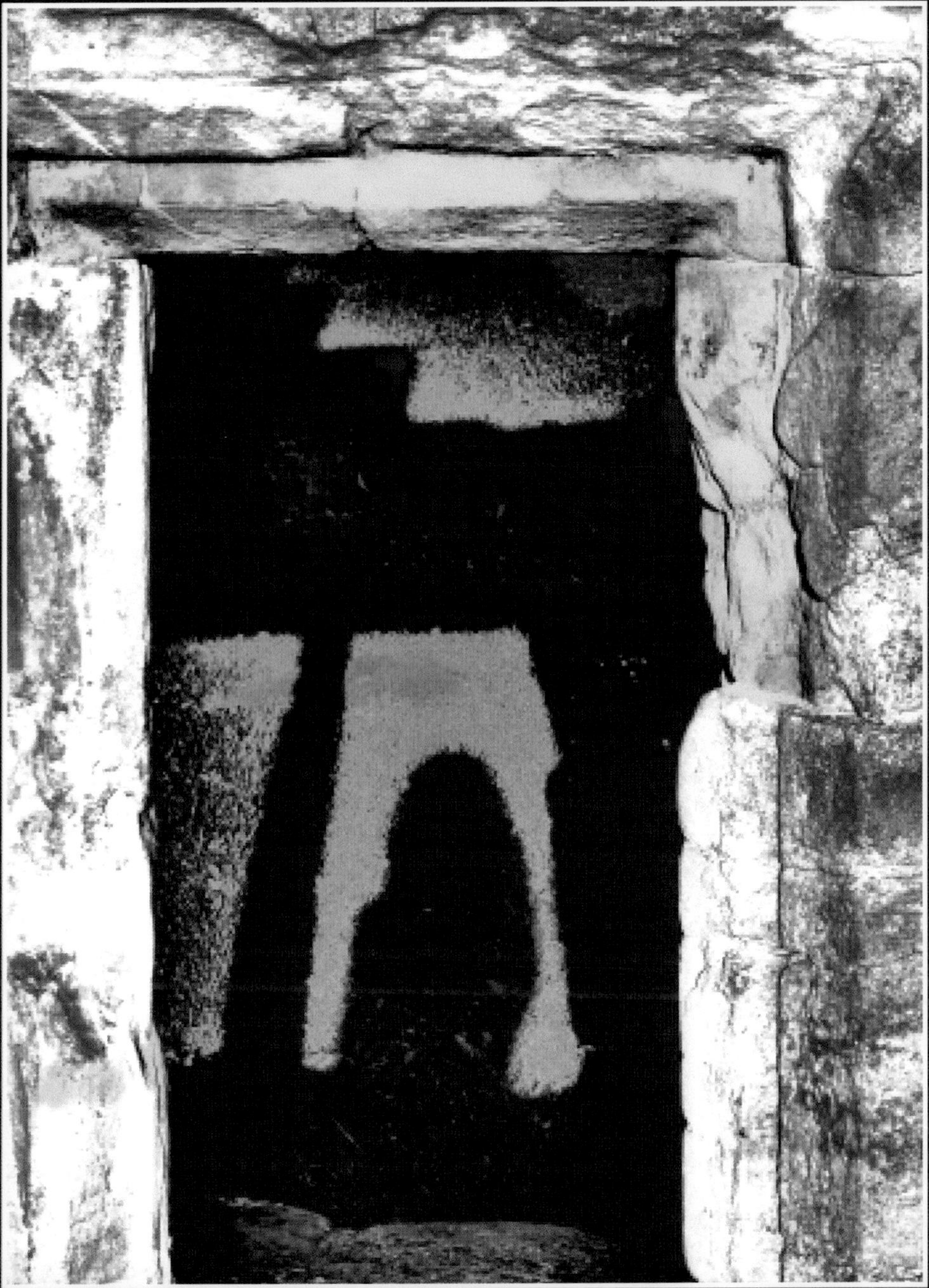

Mountain streams carve a flowing forest future,
Promising to renew the earthly potential of wonderment.
Hiker seeking solace and focus walks upon the forest floor,
Reminded of a renewed promise of their chosen passage.

Passage promise created by all to find it all within them,
Pledging to ourselves as we carve a flow through the forest of footsteps,
Those invited came because they believed in the passage promise,
Not for understanding did they walk, but for the privilege to feel the journey.

Ridge ripples over the landscape destiny of choice and consequences,
Treasuring the view of stream to pine grove bathing in the scent of a fresh start.
Promise of passage is the human landscape of unmasked self-consciousness,
A view of an ever-changing natural evolution of momentum.

Such beauty lies in wait for the skilled human hiker of promised passage,
Passage promise made to themselves and comforting companions.
For at the summit is the final rewarding step of passage,
A fulfilled promise of worth carved like a rolling stream.

Always to nourish and grow the forest of family yet to be seeded,
Ones who will walk the passage of promise in the footsteps of the hiker.
They will appear upon the ridge and see the stream and pine grove,
A smile will follow the frown, for their passage promise was made in love for them.

Passage
Promise

Dotted with castles, the land shares its fairytale magic,

Stepping across time in the vibrant landscapes of breathing postcards.

As you walk to the edge of the Loch wondering if Nessie might appear,

Bagpipes and folklore combine in street music from the festivals.

The smell of whisky and porridge lie near the breakfast bell,

People of kindness and valor greet friends most call strangers.

Oak casks line the walls of distilleries from Islay to Speyside,

Military tattoos signal the last call of duty and summon the evening.

Sheep farms offer the wool in retention of heritage and fashion,

At Burns supper the Haggis celebrate with turnips and mashed potatoes.

Beaches and mountains create a spell not even Hadrian could contain.

You see the boats in the Kirkwall waters feeling the wind twist the sea.

A small plane touches down on Orkney where beauty holds your breath.

The morning in the Highland brings a herd of sheep across your path,

Bundled-up people bracing for yet another cleansing mist to water the scene.

Bronze and Iron Ages have knocked upon the door of its history,

Kingdom of Scotland forever defiant and independent.

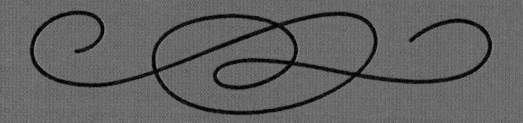

Scotland

Destiny Imagination

The adventurous mind travels back in time,
Where moments that matter begin to rhyme.
A chosen path where experiences come to rest,
Destiny imagined seeks to become the elusive best.

You shall move, imagining to hear destiny call,
Challenges increasing to keep you safe from the fall.
Never fear the trials of what could be,
It is destiny imagined which will help you see.

Some people will travel beside you along the way,
Others will lose their destiny of dreams and fall away.
You will ride imagination to a great height,
A servant to others when they desire your might.

Destiny imagined is the lining inside a life,
A lining which smooths the wrinkles of troubling strife.
You can never be alone when no others will stand,
It was your destiny imagined offering an outstretched hand.

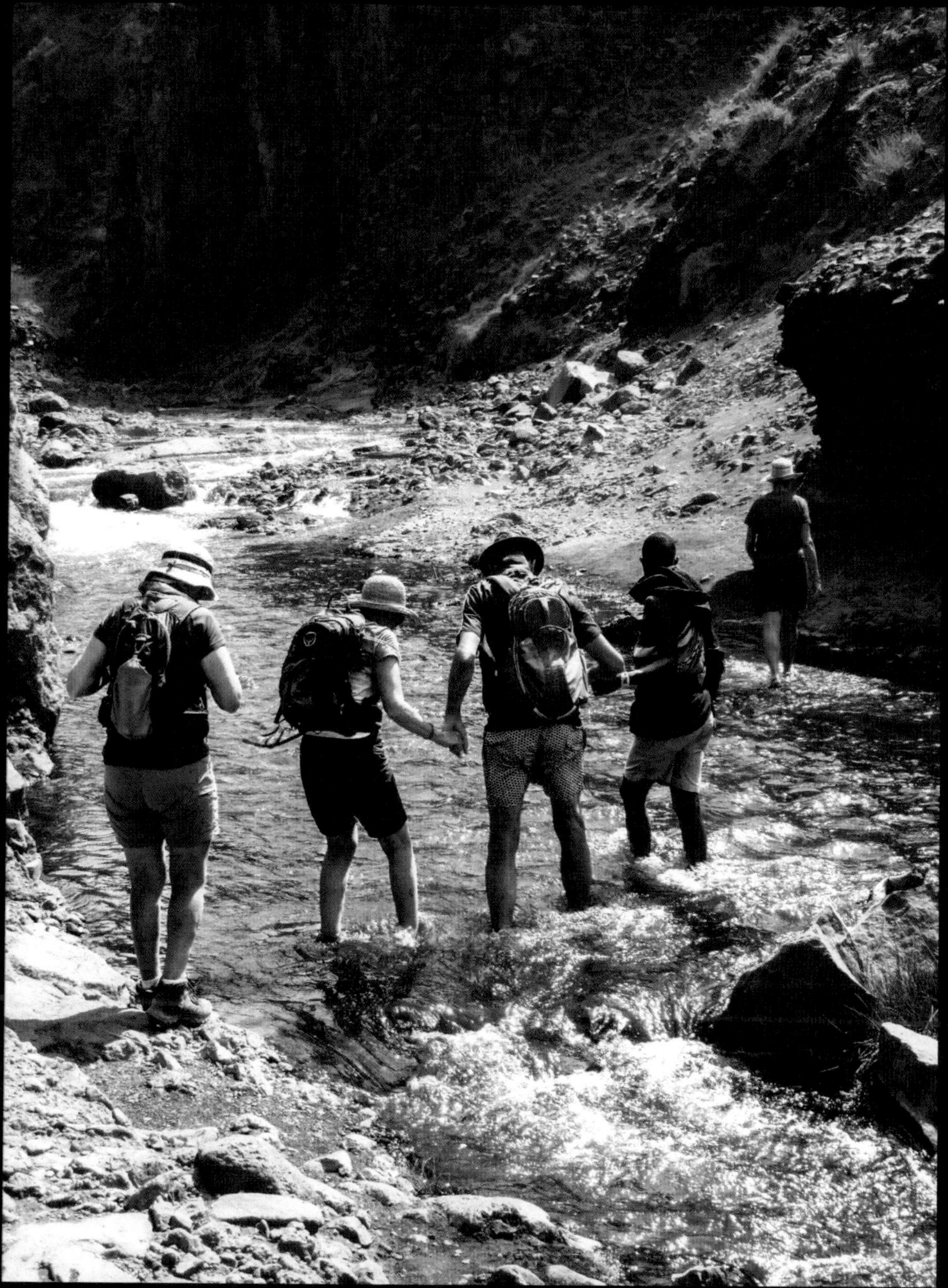

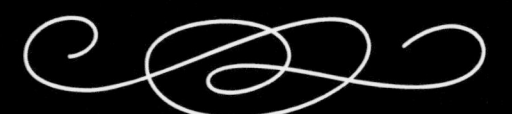

Prayers are the messages carried within cathedrals and clouds.

Longing for a response or sign, we walk to where no earthly road can go.

Floating above the dome, clouds calling us to hear the voices of angels,

Marble and gold, the proud coatings of simple singing find the meaning.

Cathedrals and clouds, the link to a timeless remembrance of devotion,

Hands held and folded into a symbol of what has yet to be sacrificed.

Quilts of guilt cast away that which is no longer needed to cover a voice,

Apostles of the "can" and the "should" preaching inside the cover of cloud.

To find a place in the dome is to ride in the cloud from above,

Where forgiveness of self is the absolute prayer to be recited.

Excuses cannot invade the dome of communicated salvation,

Believing in yourself is the beginning of the celebration.

Cathedrals and Clouds

The Grove and the Cutter

Cold spring water travels down the mountain, filling the earthen bottomed pool,

Nearby the farmhouse in need of repair resembles at night the home of a ghoul.

Serene forest surrounds the treasured grove, acting as a proud guard,

Leftover autumn leaves lie upon the grass appearing as used cards.

Deer coming cautiously into the grove trying to remain unseen,

Their family herd coming to feed and drink become calmly serene.

A row of rocks provides an ancient barrier from the fields of old,

Where hunters and farmers would rest to escape a bit of the cold.

The stillness of the grove is present even when touched by storm,

Its greatness contained in the ability to quickly transform.

The stone cutter has arrived to make off with raw field rock,

Touching the boulders to be, he seeks the ones to become his stock.

The grove welcomes the stone cutter's arrival with determined wind and rain,

A hammer and bar scrape the edges as chips fly, making a natural stain.

The stone cutter can see what will become a future fixed creation,

Lifting his stones which bear the weight, he struggles with determination.

The stone cutter knows with each piece of art he lifts to the wall,

His time with chisel, scaffold and hammer begins to feel the fall.

Time to teach the boy to learn the trade of his stone art,

With patience, he hands him the hammer to explain from the start.

He smiles as the boy strikes the stone amid the flying sparks,

Fascinated to see them focus as toil and sweat leave their marks.

The man visits the home where his first rock work lies in the fireplace,

His friend and teacher the stone cutter has gone to his resting place.

The boy, now a man, smiles recalling the lessons of the stone cutter:

"Life like stone can be shaped", the boy himself could now utter.

The Grandest Children

Loving thoughts of your children and theirs fill the heart and magnify the memory,

Lives growing and learning to walk first steps step first through the unknown.

You see the sparkle as their sounds bring refreshment to the inner self,

A park and playground of years entwined where memories abound.

A yesterday when you played with your son and daughter come into view,

Now you watch as they entertain with a similar script amid the laughter.

The grandest of children bring to focus the final stage of parent play,

Actors and creators joined in the family room where the curtain is raised.

The grandest of children hear the stories of the family tales,

Minds absorbed and hands cheering, all asking the famous why.

Those new minds with big dreams adding to the lore,

You love and listen and hope to view what's in store.

You see the wonder in their eyes dance like stars,

Powered by the energy of relentless possibilities.

Books are read and brains are fed,

A bath, a laugh, and off to bed.

Grandest of children, one generation to another closes the circle,

Each word and action a truth to them and a miracle to all.

A game of pretend lasts inside of us forever,

The grandest of children, the heirs of their greatness, own tomorrow.

You are there each morning showing family your loyalty,

It is us who see you as a regal member of canine royalty.

So many expressions appearing on your fur-faced mug,

We all come through the door eager to give you a hug.

We walk together throughout the changing seasons,

I tell you my tales of life and even ask you the reasons.

The children all pet you and later chase you around your castle,

Silly clothes and costumes you wear and bear, forgiving the hassle.

Visitors come to your kingdom, their sounds and smells make you crazy,

Waiting for them to leave to return to sleep and be lazy.

Gray has started to arrive over time upon your regal face,

No longer can you win the grandchildren race.

The kingdom mourned the day your reign came to an end,

I miss your company and counsel, my loyal friend.

Smiling when I think as a prince, as a pup, you would whirl,

Just longing to walk down the trail and perhaps chase a squirrel.

A DOG'S REIGN

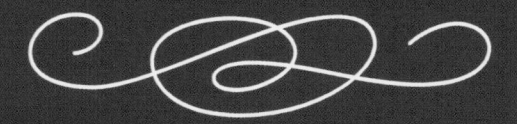

The Distance Runner

Darkness covers his frame with each stride.
Muscles and tendons his only ride.
The scent of the morning invades his senses.
Her beauty and spirit breaking down his defenses.

The dog stares as he passes by.
As birds circle and look from the sky.
His pace increases and his heart races,
Wishing to be with her in romantic places.

The miles tick off like all the years.
Missing her, the runner wipes away his tears.
The road is steeper as he increases speed.
Her touch and feel are his only needs.

The distance between them he cannot cover.
Longing for the sounds of a distant lover.
It begins to rain and the street is soaked.
Decades of family love shield like the ultimate cloak.

Dawn is breaking as does his heart.
The distance runner is from her, apart.
A small boy puts out his hand,
Hoping to touch the racing man.

Is she sleeping while he competes?
Unaware of the distance feat?
The timekeeper will track his pace.
At the finish line, he longs for her face.

That distant April changed his mind.
A moment connected to a motivational find.
The pain's a promise down his injured leg.
Where drive meets passion, his soul to beg.

Sweat and salt pour from his skin.
He carries her deep within.
Speed and sprint for a final burst.
It's not the water that will quench his thirst.

The sea sounds reach deep into the being on the beach,

Where being present to live and love invite your sound to reach.

Footprints press in the sand, there walks the owner of the sound,

Seeing sounds in yourself is where the sea screams to be found.

Rolling calmness of the sea arrives to balance the bay,

Seeing the sounds of our emotions begging to stay.

Inhaling the scent of salt air as you stop to stare,

Seeing the sounds and the essence of why you care.

Vision from within is the tide which changes direction,

Seeing sounds in the storm when life needs correction.

Even shells visit the shore to find rest from their past,

Seeing the sounds of the reason will save you at last.

See Sounds

London Speaks

"Londinium", my Roman builders called me when wagons were drawn,
So many fires sought to consume me, but I live on.
Vikings came to ravage me when the Roman Empire fell,
But even they could not conquer me or escape my spell.

A Great Plague and fire left me so few friends around,
I went from a powerful city of strength to simply a town.
Pulling myself up and squaring my shoulders to break the knot,
Financial minds of the world came to offer help, including Huguenots.

Not knowing how to move they asked to dig all around,
Let them bury their tubes and trains they call the Underground.
They even gave me a tower with armies, kings and a raven,
Some lost their head and hated it, yet some found a haven.

Look at me now! Some two thousand years later on the go,
My bridge and river meet to discuss the rain but rarely the snow.
My guests visit all my wonderful sites in black cars driven by cabbies,
They marvel at Big Ben, Parliament and even Westminster Abbey.

Most of my countrymen sadly are not titled the tipper,
Perhaps they are still afraid of that killer Jack the Ripper.
Thank you for sharing my words and thoughts from my gates,
I enjoyed these years together, my friend from the United States.

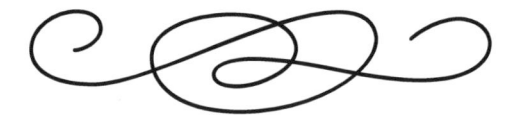

Almost Home

The frozen waves of Lake Erie roar like a winter monster from the dark,
Another lake-effect blizzard spreads a blanket of white in the park.
A stranger invited to reside there and become the merchant of change,
Adapting to understand the landscape and culture he must arrange.
Northwest Pennsylvania will teach him to understand the roam,
Bring yourself to believe you are almost home.

The Pacific Ocean can be seen from his California door,
Adventure and challenge rise up like the surf to engulf him once more.
Can the stranger manufacture the confidence to make it work?
From Venice to LA and along the coast where differences seem to lurk,
Southern California will teach him to understand the roam,
Remember to believe you are almost home.

Miami's music and color surround the stranger like the sand in an hourglass,

Asked to create what will make the complacent attend the class.

He must find a way to study this world in an upside-down time,

From Lauderdale to Miami the current is fast and the outcome prime.

Southeast Florida will teach him to understand the roam.

Just focus and believe you are almost home.

The rodeo greets the stranger in February like a wide Texas stride,

A place of ranches and cities his saddle of success must go to ride.

Houston is a city of many faces of deep diverse style,

A kindness always returned to the stranger of change with a smile.

From Austin to Dallas with Houston in between to teach him the roam,

Fatigue comes but he believes he is almost home.

New York City moves as though time is a thief on the run,

Where deals and adventure in chaos and class are spun.

He learns to quicken his game and take the chance,

Dress for the stage where the unbelievable can dance.

Throughout the Northeast their world teaches him to roam,

Perhaps this the last adaptation before being almost home.

The United Kingdom comes into view upon landing at night,

A new world filled with history, legacy and might.

In London the stranger unpacks his well-worn bag,

A merchant of change in a country that flies a proud flag.

Scotland, Wales and England teach him to roam,

Finally the journey is over, he can finally see home.

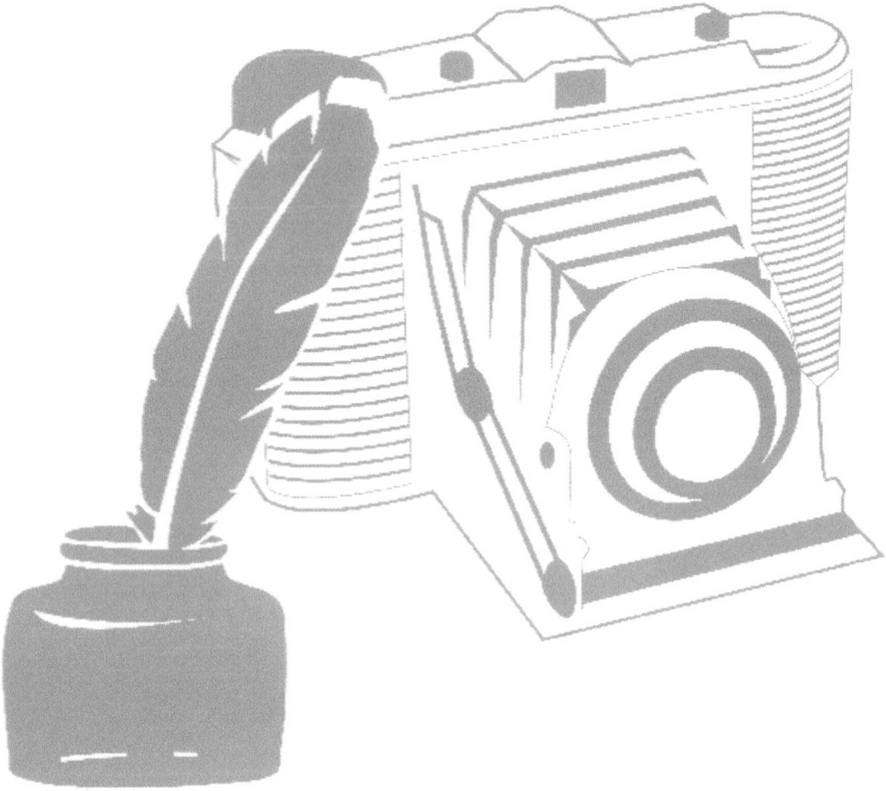

Other Books
by Anthony C. Gruppo

Pushers of the Possible

Ever wonder what it takes to be a leader in business and life? Anthony C. Gruppo, CEO of Marsh Commercial, UK, talks to business leaders who started out with a dream and the determination to build successful companies by Pushing the Possible in both life and business. Join Anthony and his guests as they share their stories, the advice they received from some of the greats, and how they Pushed the Possible in their lives. This is not just a book, it is a resource to help you define your Possible and achieve it. What advice did Bill Gates give to Barry Beck of **Bluemercury?** What did **Tom Brady say to Steve Maneri at lunch?** How did Jennifer Walsh come back stronger after misfortune? What does it take to be the CEO of your life and career?

Creating Reality: A Guide to Personal Accomplishment

This book was written to serve as your guide to develop the mindset necessary for achievement and provide insight to follow your dreams and accomplish your goals. Leadership, marketing and motivation are keys to your success and ability to lead others. In "Creating Reality", Anthony shares with his readers the forces, experiences, lessons and individuals that shaped his life and helped make him successful. Let Anthony's road map of experience, vision and unique perspective give you the direction to "Create Reality".

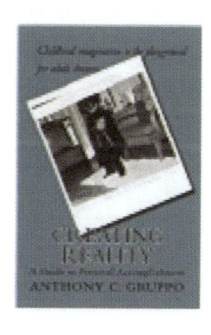

The Roots of Leadership

The Roots of Leadership is a multi-faceted journal that serves up a collection of original inspirational quotes spanning key life topics, from career and personal strategic planning, family and fellowship to self-reflection and individual-optimization. This journal's unique offering is that it enables you to deep dive into the quotes, many of which have accompanying self-reflective action items, designed to enhance their impact and create lasting, supportive outcomes. No matter where you are in your life's journey, this journal can act as a catalyst for personal change and evolution. Journaling is a practice with a long history and is shown to provide a host of benefits from stress management and improved self-discipline to increased awareness and tapping into spirituality. The Roots of Leadership Journal has the added benefit of providing you with personal guidance.

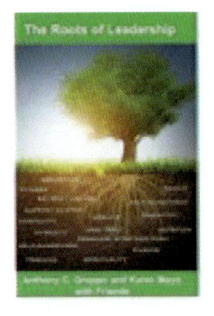

Under Construction: Welding Your Passion to Your Performance

Everyone is constantly under construction. UNDER CONSTRUCTION offers you, the reader, thoughts and concepts to consider in constructing your success. UNDER CONSTRUCTION will assist you in achieving your complete potential. It is not a book that defines success, it is a collaboration of experiences to guide you towards your personal potential and abilities. UNDER CONSTRUCTION connects us together whether our life experiences come from the boardroom, family room or locker room. Regardless of our personal arena, we are all players in the same game. Whether eight or eighty, every day we choose our opportunities by the first and last ball. In this book, you may see yourself in my stories and experiences. It is an invitation to share in our lives construction and then together achieve our personal potential. We refuse to pretend to have the answers, rather we have chosen to identify the construction sites of life and the materials necessary to engage your personal first and last balls.

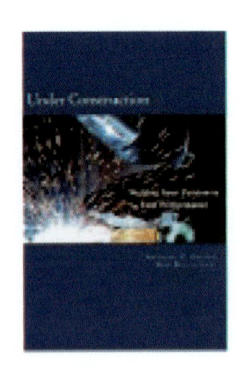

Six Degrees of Impact: Breaking Corporate Glass

Six Degrees of Impact: Breaking Corporate Glass provides perspectives and strategies for leading an environment towards positive change. The world around us is constantly changing with or without our input. Six Degrees that we all have a voice in how our environment evolves. Like having a consultant in the palm of your hand, this book provides you with short stories for each of the Six Degrees which are key to integrated change management. The Six Degrees framework is built on leadership, strategic positioning, research & development, marketing, resources and outcomes. These perspectives remove glass ceilings and provide you with a glass floor that insures both personal and professional growth. With a solid and powerful glass floor in place, you will create the long-term vision and real-life strategies necessary to achieve futuristic goals.

Creating Six Degrees - The Journal

Journal your personal path to greatness using the Six Degrees prompts of personal leadership development. This is an innovative journal allowing you to build a personal strategic plan. The journal contains original motivational quotes by the author.

The Pen & The Lens Reflection

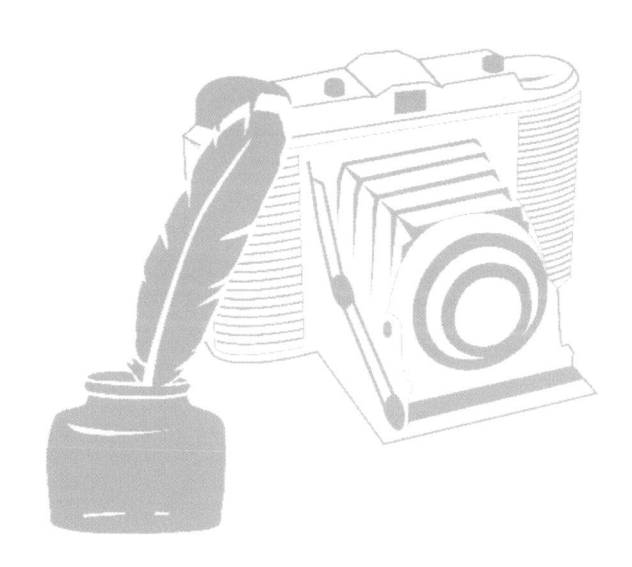

Reflection

Reflection

Reflection

Reflection

Reflection

Reflection

Reflection

Reflection

Reflection

Reflection

Reflection

Reflection

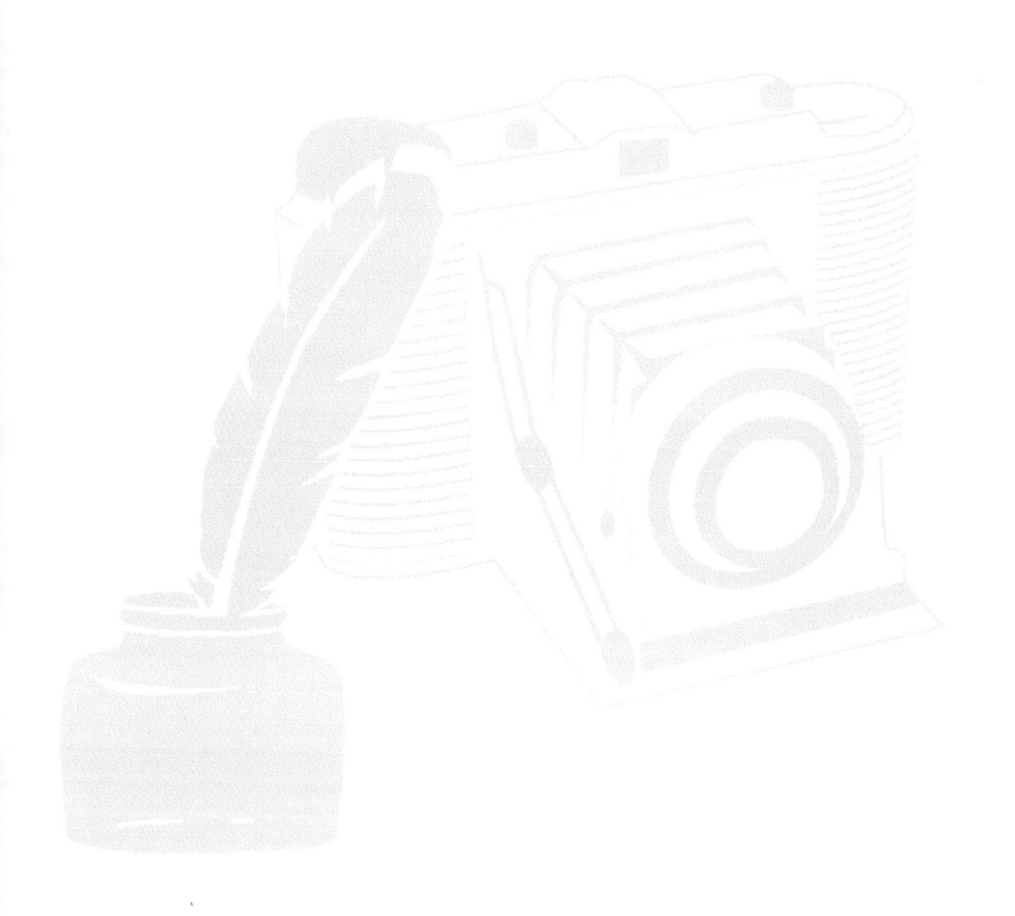

Reflection

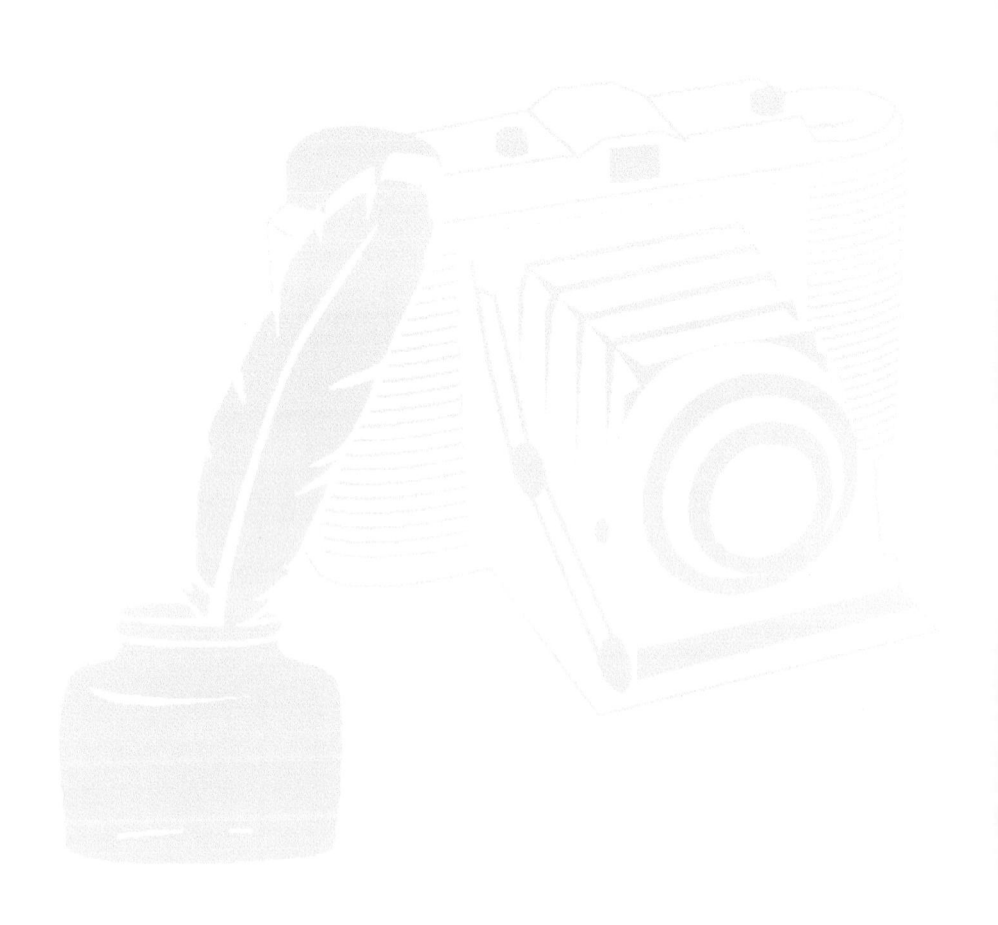

Reflection

Reflection

Reflection

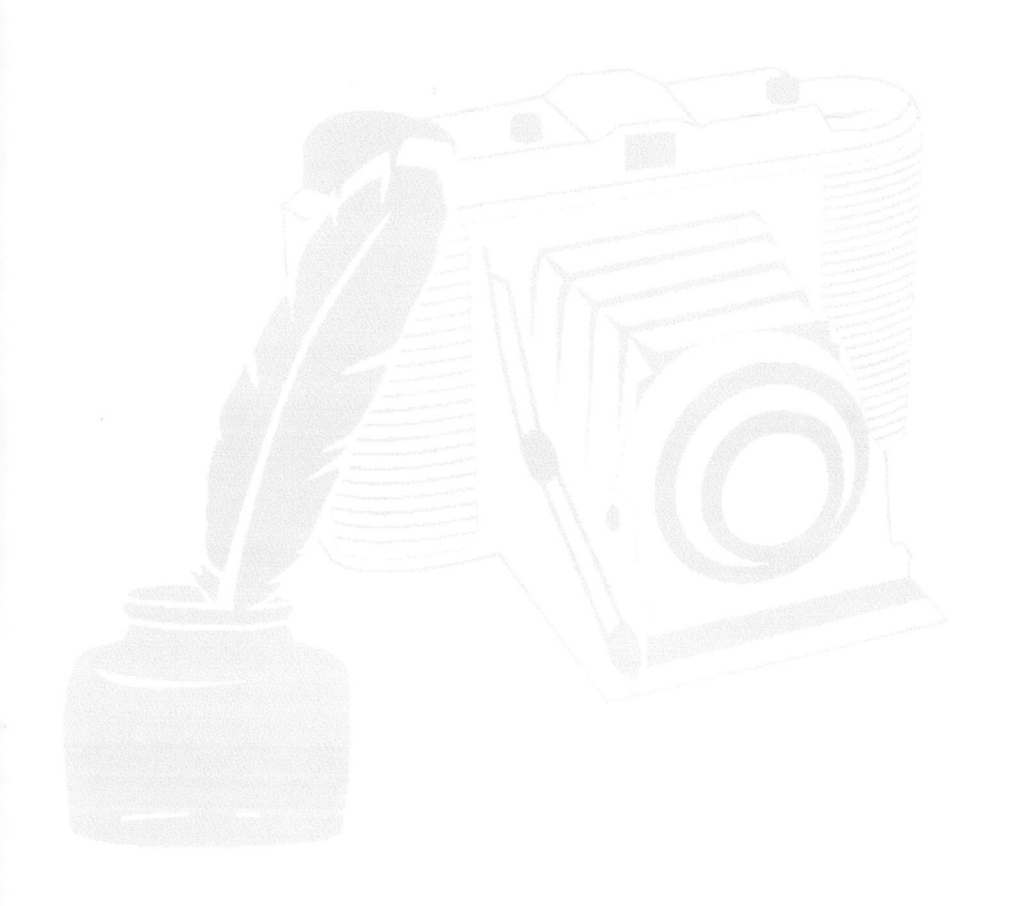

Reflection

Reflection

Reflection

Reflection

Reflection

Reflection

Printed in Great Britain
by Amazon